EXPLORING OUR SOLAR SYSTEM

GALAXIES

IMMENSE STAR ISLANDS

DAVID JEFFERIS

Crabtree Publishing Company

www.crabtreebooks.com

■ WHAT IS A GALAXY?

A galaxy is an enormous group of stars. No two galaxies are exactly the same, but they do have various common shapes.

The spiral-shaped Andromeda galaxy is much bigger than our own Milky Way. It is 2.5 million **light years** from Earth.

■ WHAT SIZE IS A GALAXY?

The smallest of all are called dwarf galaxies, and these may contain as little as 10 million stars. Our own galaxy, the Milky Way, is average size, with about 200–400 billion stars. The exact number is not known, because much of the Milky Way is hidden from view, behind huge banks of gas and dust.

The Andromeda galaxy is by far the biggest galaxy nearby. Scientists think it contains at least 1,000 billion stars.

WOW!
Space is so huge that distances are measured in light years. This is the distance that light travels in a year, or 5.9 trillion miles (10 trillion km).

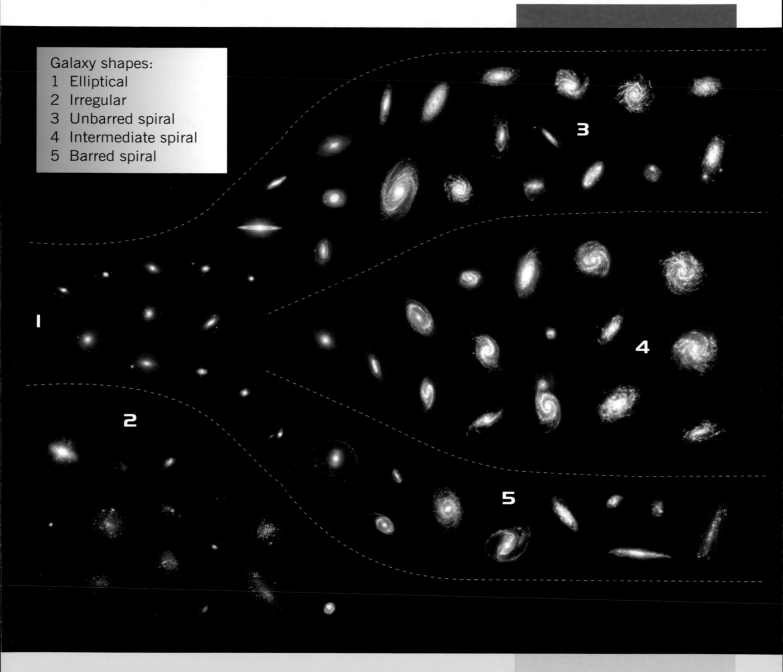

Galaxy shapes:
1 Elliptical
2 Irregular
3 Unbarred spiral
4 Intermediate spiral
5 Barred spiral

■ WHAT SHAPE ARE MOST GALAXIES?

Galaxies fall into three basic shapes: elliptical, spiral, and irregular. However, just like snowflakes, no two galaxies are identical. Each one is slightly different.

■ WHAT ABOUT OTHER SHAPES?

Galaxies that do not fall into these general groups are called peculiars. They include ring galaxies, and ones that have been twisted out of shape due to collisions with other galaxies.

Galaxy shapes are grouped according to the "tuning fork" diagram created by the U.S. astronomer, Edwin Hubble, in 1936.

Spiral galaxies are full of new stars, formed largely from **hydrogen** gas. Older ellipticals have fewer new stars, because a lot of their hydrogen has been used up.

■WHERE DID GALAXIES COME FROM?

Astronomers think galaxies formed some time after the "**Big Bang**," or the mighty explosion believed to have formed our universe.

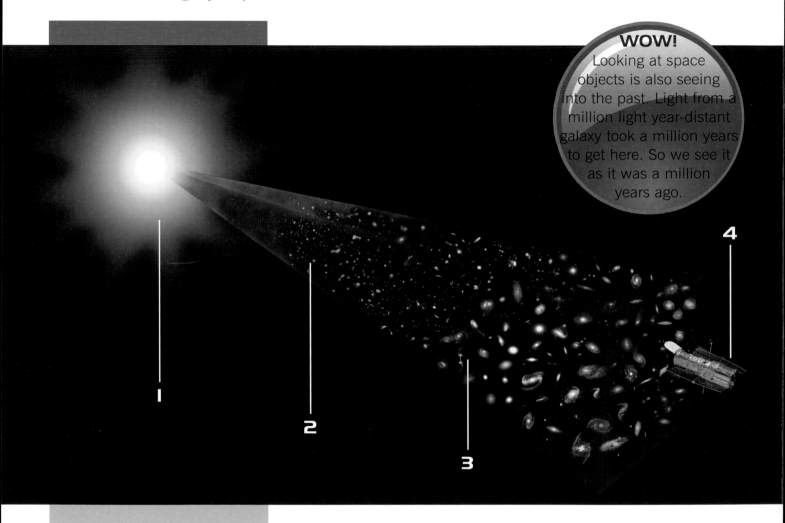

WOW!
Looking at space objects is also seeing into the past. Light from a million light year-distant galaxy took a million years to get here. So we see it as it was a million years ago.

■ Our universe formed from the Big Bang (1). The first galaxies (2) formed shortly after this. Over billions of years, clusters of galaxies (3) formed. Today, we see them with instruments such as the Hubble Space Telescope (4).

■ HOW OLD IS THE UNIVERSE?

Most scientists think that the Big Bang took place about 13.7 billion years ago. The first elements in the early universe were hydrogen and helium. All stars are made mostly of these, with small amounts of other elements. Using powerful telescopes, astronomers can see that many galaxies were being formed just 100 million years after the Big Bang.

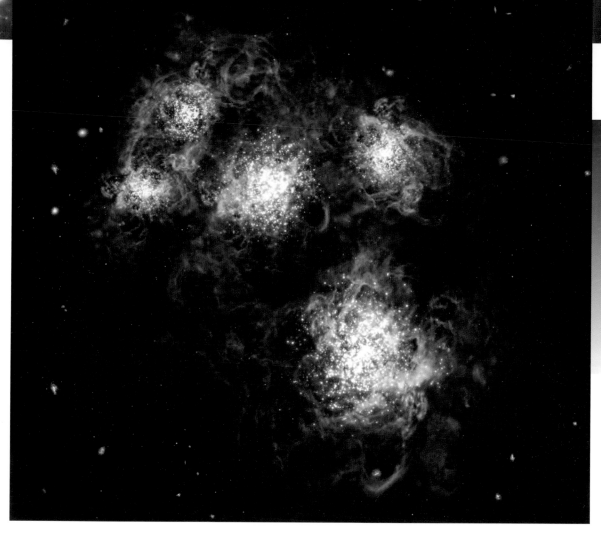

■ This picture shows what an early galaxy may have looked like. Buried deep in clouds of hydrogen and helium gases, young stars are forming in huge groups.

■ WHAT DID THE EARLIEST GALAXIES LOOK LIKE?

We do not know what the earliest galaxies looked like. It is likely that early stars formed as they do today. Gases in space collected and thickened, and once they started doing this, **gravity** took over, pulling in more matter to form young stars. Eventually, these first stars began to glow with heat and light.

■ WHAT IS DARK MATTER?

Dark matter and energy are mystery forces that make up most of the universe. We cannot see them, but we can detect their presence. In fact, the stars and galaxies we can see in space make up just four percent of what we think is out there!

■ This image shows a twisted ring of dark matter. Its gravity is distorting the light coming from a group of distant galaxies.

■ HOW BIG IS THE MILKY WAY GALAXY?

The Milky Way is only an average-sized galaxy, but it is still huge. It measures 100,000 light years across.

■ WHAT SHAPE IS THE MILKY WAY?

It looks much like a very slowly rotating pinwheel, with a **core** region that is packed tightly with stars. These cluster across the middle as a fuzzy bar, or crosspiece, so the Milky Way is called a barred spiral galaxy.

You can see the Milky Way on a clear night. It is a pale band of light across the sky. What you cannot see is its spiral shape. This can only be seen in pictures or from a spacecraft many light years away. The name "Milky Way" comes from the time of ancient Rome, and the Latin words *Via Lacteum*.

■ ARE WE LOCATED IN THE MIDDLE OF THE GALAXY?

No—the **solar system** is in an outer part of the Milky Way, called the Orion arm. We live in a galactic "suburb," about 25,000 light years from the core.

To get an idea of just how big the Milky Way is, you need a feel for how distances compare in the solar system and nearby space. Light from our closest space object, the Moon, takes about 1.5 seconds to reach Earth. Light from the Sun takes about 8 minutes to get here. Light from the nearest star beyond the solar system makes a huge jump in space and time—it takes 4.2 years to arrive. But to cross the Milky Way from side to side, a light ray has to travel for 100,000 years!

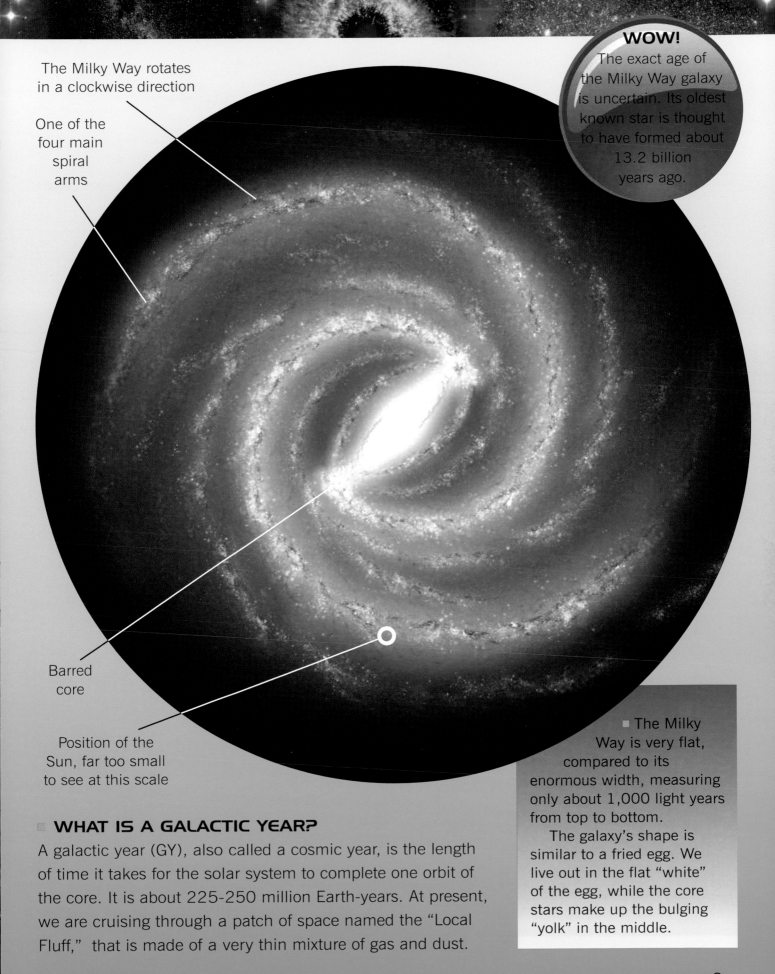

The Milky Way rotates in a clockwise direction

One of the four main spiral arms

Barred core

Position of the Sun, far too small to see at this scale

WHAT IS A GALACTIC YEAR?

A galactic year (GY), also called a cosmic year, is the length of time it takes for the solar system to complete one orbit of the core. It is about 225-250 million Earth-years. At present, we are cruising through a patch of space named the "Local Fluff," that is made of a very thin mixture of gas and dust.

■ The Milky Way is very flat, compared to its enormous width, measuring only about 1,000 light years from top to bottom.

The galaxy's shape is similar to a fried egg. We live out in the flat "white" of the egg, while the core stars make up the bulging "yolk" in the middle.

WHERE ARE THE MILKY WAY'S STARS FORMED?

The first stars formed in the core, before the galaxy had flattened out to its present spiral shape. Today, most stars form in the spiral arms.

These two pictures of the 5,400 light year-distant Trifid **nebula** show how instruments can reveal various details of the same space object.

The left picture (1) is taken in "visible" light, and is what we can see with our eyes. The same view (2) uses equipment that gives us a closer look at the nebula.

WHAT DOES A STAR-FORMING REGION LOOK LIKE?

Stars form in giant clouds of gas and dust, called nebulas. They all look different, with shapes created by random forces in their part of space. Many nebulas glow brightly with the fierce light of young stars.

WOW!
Among the Spitzer telescope's discoveries is the youngest star so far known. The star L1014 is just 652 light years away, and might be only 10,000 years old.

DO OLD AND NEW STARS LOOK DIFFERENT?

Older stars are mostly cool and red. Pictures of the Milky Way's core region—the "yolk of the egg"—show millions of these old stars. Young stars look very different. They are often found in clusters, deep inside a nebula. They burn an intensely hot blue-white color.

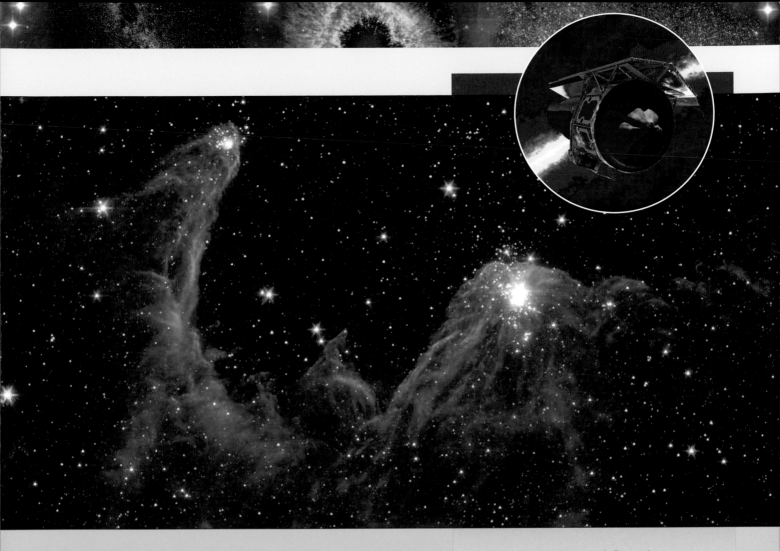

WHAT ARE THE "MOUNTAINS OF CREATION?"

These are giant columns of cool gas and dust. They are 7,000 light years from Earth. Hundreds of stars form here. The name was given by scientists working with the U.S. Spitzer Space Telescope (see top right), an instrument that uses infrared light to penetrate through dust to see what lies inside. Many of the pictures in this book were take by the Spitzer.

■ The Mountains of Creation are huge. They spread across 50 light years of space. The red color shows the presence of **carbon**, the same material that forms the building blocks of life on Earth.

■ The Rho Ophiuchi dark cloud is one of the closest star-forming places to Earth. It is 470 light years away. Many of the stars formed here are "babies." They are about 300,000 years old!

▪WHAT KINDS OF NEBULA ARE IN OUR GALAXY?

The Milky Way is a place of gas, dust, young stars, and old stars. Nebulas mark where stars are being formed, and also where they have exploded.

▪ The Rosette nebula is more than 5,000 light years away, and is full of young stars. The Rosette is an emission nebula. Its electrified gases give off their own light.

▪ ARE THERE DIFFERENT KINDS OF NEBULA?

Yes, there are several kinds. Reflection nebulas are clouds of dust and gas that reflect the light of nearby stars. Emission nebulas are ones where the gases actually glow.

▪ HOW DO GASES START GLOWING?

Gases glow when star radiation is strong enough to turn the gases into an electrically-charged cloud, called a **plasma**. Then the gases glow like a fluorescent light bulb.

WOW!
Radiation from stars comes in many forms. Some we can see as light. Infrared is heat radiation. Other types include x-rays and radio waves.

■ HOW DOES A PLANETARY NEBULA MARK WHERE A STAR HAS EXPLODED?

A planetary nebula is actually a fast-expanding cloud of gas and dust. This cloud is blown into space by some big stars when they explode at the end of their lives. This explosion is called a **supernova**. Planetary nebulas are usually a plasma. They glow with their own light, but they last only a few thousand years before fading from view.

☐ The gases of the Helix planetary nebula are now about 2.5 light years across, and mark where a star blew up over 10,000 years ago.

Planetary nebulas have nothing to do with planets. They were called this because they looked like planets, through the low-powered telescopes used by early astronomers.

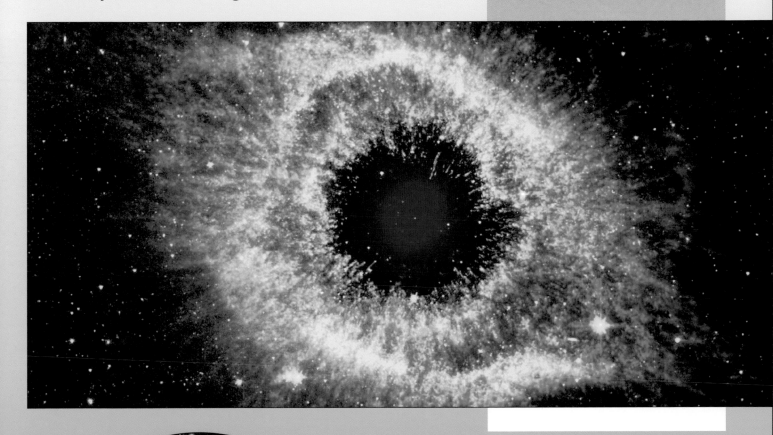

☐ The dark patch in this picture of the southern Milky Way shows the Coalsack dark nebula. It is not totally black. It does reflect a little light from nearby stars.

■ WHAT ARE DARK NEBULAS?

These are thick, cool clouds of dust and gas. They do not glow with light. Instead, they simply cover up the stars behind them. There are also many small dark nebulas called Bok globules.

WHAT LIES IN THE CORE OF THE MILKY WAY?

The core of the Milky Way is filled with closely-packed stars. Scientists think there is a **black hole** in the middle of the core.

■ The Milky Way's barred core is about 27,000 light years across.

It is an area filled with old, red stars. They were formed in the early period of the Milky Way's formation, more than thirteen billion years ago.

■ WHAT IS A BLACK HOLE?

Black holes are incredibly dense points of matter, whose super-strong gravity prevents even light from escaping, which is how they get their name. The smallest black holes known have about ten times as much **mass**, or matter, as the Sun. Black holes in galactic cores are millions of times the mass of the Sun and lie deep in the center of almost all big galaxies. They are called supermassive black holes.

■ IS A BLACK HOLE VERY DANGEROUS?

Yes, if you are too close. A black hole's intense gravity sucks in anything nearby including dust, gas, stars, and planets.

WOW!
Surrounding the Milky Way's central black hole are thousands of young stars. They were formed from some of the gases that are being fed constantly into the hole.

■ WHY IS THE DOUBLE HELIX NEBULA SPIRAL SHAPED?

Its twisted strings of gas are probably made by very strong magnetic fields. These are thought to be generated by high-speed gases, swirling around the nearby supermassive black hole at the Milky Way's core.

■ The Double Helix nebula (top) lies just 300 light years from the black hole at the galaxy's core.

■ The Milky Way's central black hole (left) is fed by a spinning disc of material from stars drawn toward it. The black hole is thought to have a mass millions of times greater than the Sun.

15 ■

■HOW BIG IS THE GALACTIC HALO?

The main body of the Milky Way is a flattened disk, rotating around a round core. Outside of this is an outer area called the **galactic halo**.

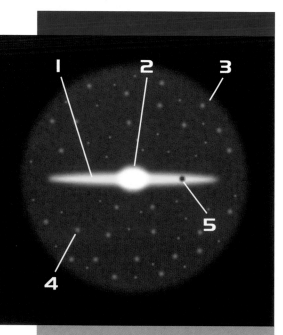

A view of the Milky Way's edge shows the disk (1) and bulging core (2), surrounded by the huge ball-shaped halo (3). Globular star clusters (4) are dotted throughout the halo.

The solar system (5) is in a spiral arm, about half-way between the Milky Way's core and its outer rim.

■ The globular cluster M80 is 32,600 light years from Earth. It contains more than 100,000 stars. Among them are blue, yellow, and red "stragglers." These are hot stars that spin 75 times faster than the Sun.

■ WHAT OBJECTS ARE IN THE GALAXY'S HALO?

The halo contains more than 150 **globular clusters**. These are ball-shaped groups of stars, dotted through the halo, above and below the disk of the Milky Way. Other galaxies have clusters, too. Scientists think Andromeda may have more than 500 of them, and the elliptical galaxy M87 is thought to have 10,000 or more. Globular clusters are made of mostly very old stars, with sizes ranging from less than 100,000 stars to more than a million.

■ DO CLUSTER STARS HAVE PLANETS?

It is thought unlikely that there are many, because stars in a globular cluster are so close together. Their gravity would probably dislodge most planets in a fairly short time.

The M80 cluster is 95 light years across

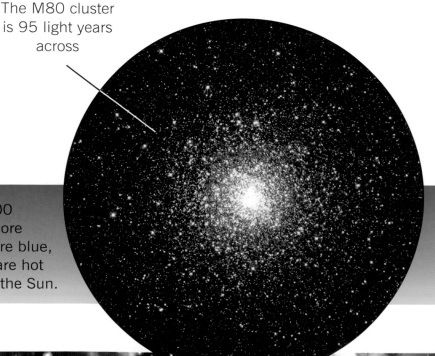

■ Three star streams (1,2,3) circle the galaxy between 13,000 and 130,000 light years away. Their stars move through space at about 300 miles per second (480 km/sec).

Such stars were once packed closely, but today they are light years apart.

The furthest stream (1) is all that remains of a dwarf companion galaxy. There may be many more fainter star streams looping around the Milky Way like long strands of spaghetti.

■ WHAT ARE GALACTIC STAR STREAMS?

They are the remains of smaller galaxies and star clusters near the Milky Way. Over billions of years, the Milky Way's gravity has ripped them apart. Now, the individual stars circle around the galaxy in long, glowing streams. Less than 200 globular clusters survive today. There may have been thousands at one time.

■WHAT IS THE LOCAL GROUP?

Just as stars often cluster together in groups, so do galaxies.
The **Local Group** has three main galaxies, plus many smaller ones.

■ In reality, the Andromeda galaxy is not bright pink. The color in this picture brings out more detail than normal. The arms of Andromeda contain stars, gas, and dust. In the core zone (right), there are billions of tightly-packed stars.

■ HOW MANY GALAXIES ARE IN THE LOCAL GROUP?

There are nearly 40 nearby galaxies, but only three of them are really big: the Milky Way, Andromeda, and Triangulum.

▢ WHICH IS THE BIGGEST GALAXY IN THE LOCAL GROUP?

This is the 2.5 million light year-distant Andromeda galaxy, also known by its star catalogue number M31. Like the Milky Way, Andromeda is a barred spiral, but it is much larger. It contains about 1,000 billion stars. Our own galaxy is now forming new stars at a much higher rate even than Andromeda!

□ Triangulum (far left) may also have a **satellite** galaxy, called Pisces Dwarf (arrowed). This is an irregular galaxy that is heading toward the Milky Way at about 180 miles per second (287 km/sec).

WOW!
Everything in space moves including giant clouds of hydrogen gas. Smith's Cloud is 10,000 light years long, and is heading towards the Milky Way.

■ HOW FAR AWAY IS THE TRIANGULUM GALAXY?

The smallest of the three main Local Group galaxies is about three million light years away. It is the only spiral galaxy. The others are barred spiral, elliptical, or irregular.

■ HOW MUCH SPACE DOES THE LOCAL GROUP COVER?

It is a peanut-shaped area ten million light years across. The Local Group is just one among many other star groups in the enormous Virgo Supercluster.

■ The Milky Way has a system of satellite galaxies surrounding it. Two of these are the Large and Small Magellanic Clouds (right), seen here with the glowing band of the Milky Way. The Magellanic Clouds are easily visible in southern skies.

Large Magellanic Cloud

Small Magellanic Cloud

■CAN GALAXIES COLLIDE?

Everything in space is in constant motion, including galaxies. Sometimes their movements set them on a collision course.

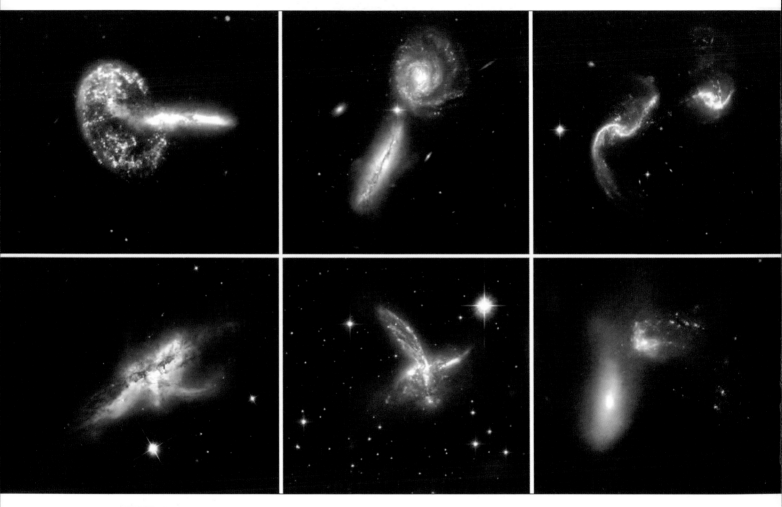

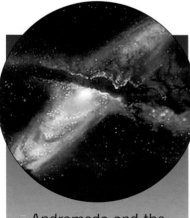

Andromeda and the Milky Way could look like this if they collide.

■ WHAT HAPPENS WHEN GALAXIES COLLIDE?

Each collision is different. Sometimes galaxies are moving fast enough to pass completely through each other. Often, galaxies merge together after a collision to form a single, bigger galaxy.

■ WHAT IS A CANNIBAL GALAXY?

It is a galaxy whose gravity is pulling material away from another one. Our own Milky Way is such a galaxy, because it is sucking hydrogen gas from the Large and Small Magellanic Clouds.

■ These pictures show a dozen galactic collisions. The results range from galaxies that merge together, to ones that are simply ripped apart. Galaxies look almost solid at this scale. Except in the core zones, most stars are far apart, and would not be affected by a collision. If you could shrink the Sun to the size of a small coin, then Alpha Centauri, the nearest star system to the solar system, would be nearly 500 miles (800 km away)!

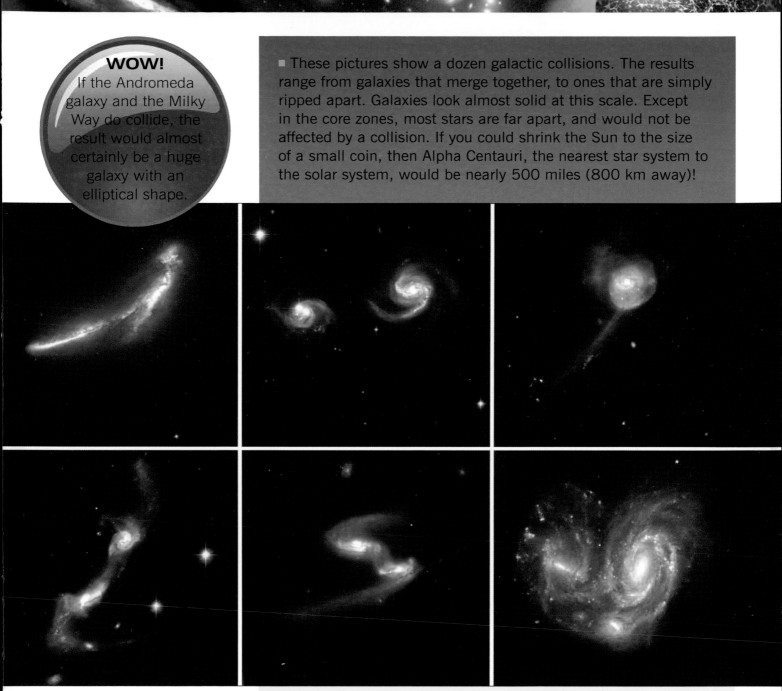

■ WILL THE MILKY WAY COLLIDE WITH ANOTHER GALAXY?

The Andromeda galaxy is heading toward the Milky Way at 75 miles per second (120 km/sec). If it continues to head this way, then there could be a collision between the galaxies. This will not happen for another 3 billion years!

■ WOULD A COLLISION BE A DANGER TO THE SOLAR SYSTEM?

It is unlikely that another star would hit the Sun or planets, because distances between stars are so great. There is plenty of room for them to pass each other.

■WHAT IS AN ACTIVE GALAXY?

An active galaxy is one that pours out massive amounts of radiation. The energy comes from the supermassive black hole at its core.

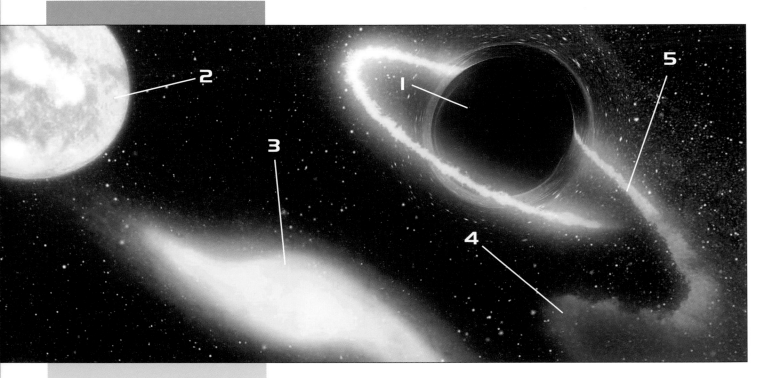

■ A black hole (1) becomes more massive in stages. First, a star approaches closely (2). Then the black hole's gravity sucks away the star's outer gases (3). The gases fall toward the black hole and whirl around it (4), to form an accretion disc (5).

■ WHAT IS AN ACCRETION DISK?

It is the fast-spinning disk of material surrounding a galaxy's central black hole, which pulls in gas and dust from surrounding space. The falling material heats up as it gets closer, and eventually the disk gives off enormous energy.

WOW!
Active galaxies are the brightest objects in the universe. It is thought that in the distant future, all matter in a galaxy may eventually fall into its supermassive black hole.

■ WHAT IS A BLACK HOLE JET?

Sometimes the energy in an **accretion disk** creates super-powerful twin jets of radiation, such as radio waves, X-rays, heat, and light, which beam out far into space. The black hole region that gives off such a jet is called an **Active Galactic Nucleus** (**AGN**). The Milky Way has a supermassive black hole at its core, but does not have radiation jets.

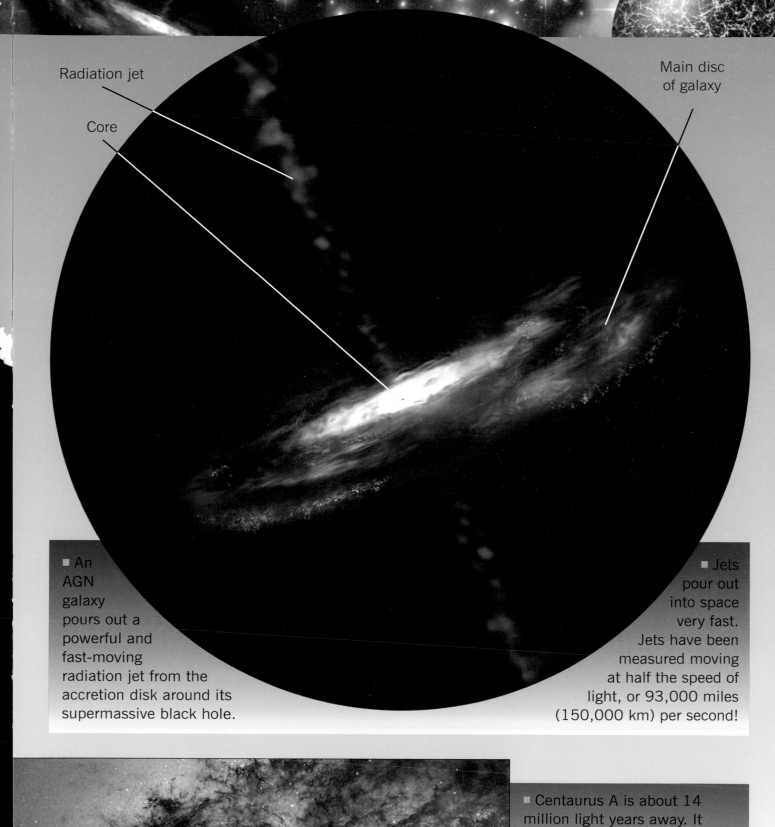

Radiation jet

Core

Main disc
of galaxy

■ An AGN galaxy pours out a powerful and fast-moving radiation jet from the accretion disk around its supermassive black hole.

■ Jets pour out into space very fast. Jets have been measured moving at half the speed of light, or 93,000 miles (150,000 km) per second!

■ Centaurus A is about 14 million light years away. It is called a **starburst galaxy**, as there are many new stars being formed there. Centaurus A also has a huge radiation jet, powered by the supermassive black hole at its core.

HOW MANY GALAXIES ARE THERE?

The best estimates put the number at 100 billion galaxies.
They are scattered throughout space as far as telescopes can see.

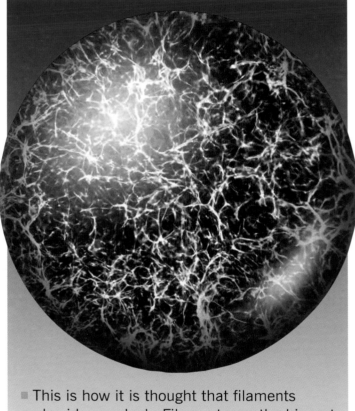

■ This is how it is thought that filaments and voids may look. Filaments are the biggest known structures in the universe, each one being about 150–250 million light years long. Walls are flattened filaments, like huge sheets of galaxies, hanging in space.

■ WHAT ARE GALACTIC FILAMENTS AND VOIDS?

These are the names for the largest-known groups of galaxies. Stars group in galaxies, and galaxies group in clusters. Galactic clusters group in long, web-like filaments and huge sheets. They are made up of millions of galaxies. Between them are enormous empty spaces called voids.

■ HOW BIG IS A VOID?

They come in various sizes, but one of the biggest known is called the Capricornus void. This huge area of completely empty space is believed to stretch across a distance of more than 230 million light years.

WOW!
We are living in a star formation age that is expected to last for another 100 billion years. Once all the hydrogen is used up, no more stars can be formed.

■ WHAT IS THE GREAT ATTRACTOR?

This is a mysterious "thing" about 250 million light years away. It is huge. It is more massive than 10,000 Milky Way-size galaxies. The Great Attractor's huge gravity is pulling nearby galaxies toward it, but we cannot study it properly because it lies directly behind our galaxy's core zone. So gas, dust, and the core stars obscure our vision of the Great Attractor, making observation difficult.

■ WHAT IS ABELL 1689?

This is one of the largest-known galactic clusters. It lies 2.2 billion light years away. Abell's gravity is so strong that it bends light, allowing galaxies even further away to appear as colored streaks around it.

■ Everywhere we look, there are galaxies. There are far too many to count them accurately. This view of the Abell 1689 cluster shows galaxies more than 13 billion light years away. They show here as colored streaks (arrowed), bent around Abell 1689 by its intense gravity.

■ In the future, galaxies will eventually run out of hydrogen gas, the fuel needed for new stars to form. The universe will be dark and dim, lit only by the red glow of slowly dying stars.

■WHAT GALAXIES CAN I SEE AT NIGHT?

Only a few galaxies are bright enough to see with the naked eye.
You can make a good start by looking at our own galaxy, the Milky Way.

■ WHAT EQUIPMENT DO I NEED FOR MILKY WAY SPOTTING?

You really do not need anything more than good eyesight to go galaxy spotting. The Milky Way is a huge pale band across the sky, and from southern parts of the world the Magellanic Clouds are easily visible, too. A pair of binoculars is useful for looking at faint galaxies and the stars and nebulas of our own galaxy.

■ WHERE ARE THE BEST VIEWING POINTS?

You need a clear, dark sky. This can be a problem if you live in a town where street lights drown out faint stars and much of the Milky Way. For best viewing, a trip to the countryside is the only answer, because nights are darker there. Then you will be able to see the Milky Way easily, as well some other galaxies further away.

■ The Andromeda galaxy M31 is 2.5 million light years away, making it the furthest object you can see with the naked eye.

You can find M31 as a faint smudge by first finding the **constellation** Cassiopeia (1 above). Follow the two stars in the "w" to find M31 (2) below it.

■ Seen through a powerful telescope (left), M31 is an amazing object, surrounded by globular clusters.

■ The Big Dipper (1) can be your guide to the galaxies M81 and M82 (2). M81 is a spiral galaxy, M82 is its distant neighbor in space.

■ M82 (arrowed) is a starburst galaxy. It is forming new stars at a much higher rate than usual.

WHAT DO GALAXIES LOOK LIKE?

The spectacular pictures in this book were made with the latest equipment, and the "real thing" is not as impressive. In reality, galaxies appear only as faint blotches of light. However, it is great to get out and take in the sheer wonder of the night skies, even if the view is not as dramatic as the results from space telescopes.

WHAT IS NIGHT SIGHT?

Your eyes become more sensitive to light as they adjust to the lower levels of light at night. After 20 minutes or so, you'll be amazed at how much more you can see. A good trick is to look slightly to one side of a space object. As odd as it sounds, your eyes can see slightly better if you do this. This method also works if you are looking through binoculars or a small telescope.

WOW!
The Magellanic Clouds are 75,000 light years apart. It is quite close as galaxy distances go! They have been twisted out of shape by the Milky Way's gravity.

☐ The nearby Magellanic Clouds are a familiar sight in southern skies. They are both irregular

■ FACTS AND FIGURES

■ HOW MANY STARS AND GALAXIES DOES THE UNIVERSE CONTAIN?

The answer is that we do not know for sure, but there are a many! The Milky Way galaxy, which is about average size, contains 200 to 400 billion stars. Research shows that there are at least 100 billion galaxies. So the total number of stars out there could be something like this: 10,000,000,000,000,000,000,000,000!

■ WHAT IS THE BIGGEST GALAXY?

The largest one on record is called IC1101. It is more than one billion light years away. It is thought to be six million light years across and contains 4,000 billion stars. The smallest galaxy known is 120,000 light years away and is called Willman 1. No one is certain but it could be just a globular cluster.

■ MILKY WAY GALAXY FACTS

1 **Shape:**
   Barred spiral galaxy, type SBbc
2 **Width across the spiral arms:**
   100,000 light years
3 **Depth of the galactic disc:**
   1,000 light years for stars,
   more for gas and dust
4 **Number of stars in the Milky Way:**
   200–400 billion
5 **Most common stars:**
   Small, dim, red dwarf stars
6 **Oldest stars:**
   About 13.2 billion years
7 **Sun's distance from galactic core:**
   About 26,000 light years
8 **Mass of central black hole:**
   About 10 million times that
   of the Sun
9 **Galactic rotation (Cosmic Year):**
   About 220 million Earth-years
10 **Barred core rotation period:**
   15–18 million years

■ BLACK HOLE GALAXIES

Black holes are now thought to be in the middle of almost all galaxies, even those without a central bulge (right).

It is thought that what allows "thin" galaxies like these to have a black hole is dark matter, the invisible substance that makes up most of the universe.

NEAREST GALAXIES

These galaxies are all members of the Local Group, and are satellites of the Milky Way. The list is of objects that we can see. There may be others lurking on the far side of the Milky Way, hidden by the core zone. Distances shown are in light years.

	Name	Distance
1	Canis Major Dwarf	25,000
2	Sagittarius Dwarf	81,000
3	Large Magellanic Cloud	163,000
4	Bootes Dwarf	197,000
5	Small Magellanic Cloud	206,000
6	Ursa Minor Dwarf	206,000
7	Draco Dwarf	258,000
8	Sextans Dwarf	281,000
9	Sculptor Dwarf	287,000
10	Ursa Major 1 Dwarf	330,000

THE MOST MASSIVE BLACK HOLE

Galaxy M104 is also known as the Sombrero galaxy, because its huge dust ring makes it look a bit like a Mexican hat.

M104 is an unbarred spiral, with a core containing a supermassive black hole, believed to be one billion times the Sun's mass. This makes it the most massive black hole we have measured in a nearby galaxy.

The term "nearby" is actually a great distance. The Sombrero galaxy is nearly 30 million light years away.

WHAT IS A MESSIER OBJECT?

Charles Messier (1730-1817) was a French astronomer who made a list of space objects such as nebulas and star clusters. Each one is numbered (for example, M81, M104). They are all known as "Messier objects."

■GLOSSARY

Here are explanations for many of the terms used in this book.

□ An AGN pours out massive amounts of radiation into space.

Accretion disk A disk of dust and gas that circles a high-gravity object such as a black hole.

AGN Active Galactic Nucleus — a region in the middle of a galaxy that radiates very brightly. Thought to be the result of radiation formed on the accretion disk of a supermassive black hole. An active galaxy is one with an AGN at its core.

Big Bang Name of the possible event that gave birth to the universe, about 13.7 billion years ago.

Black hole A space object with gravity so strong that even light cannot escape from it.

Carbon An element created in stars, and one that is the basic building block of life on Earth. It occurs in space in carbon-rich gas and dust clouds.

Constellation One of 88 star patterns in the sky, mostly named by the ancient Greeks and Romans.

Core The heart of a galaxy made of tight-packed stars. In the middle is usually a supermassive black hole.

Dark matter Invisible substance that is thought, along with dark energy, to make up most of the universe. Although it cannot be seen, dark matter's gravity affects space objects, so its presence can be detected.

Galactic halo A huge, spherical space zone around a galaxy.

Globular cluster Spherical group of stars, orbiting in a galactic halo. It may contain as many as a million stars.

Gravity The force of attraction between all objects. Massive objects have a stronger gravitational pull than smaller ones.

Hydrogen The most common substance in the universe and the most important part of a star's makeup. The second most common substance is helium, and this is the next most common part of a star.

Light year The distance that light covers in a year, traveling at a speed of 186,000 miles per second (300,000 km/sec).

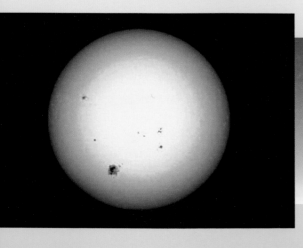

■ Stars are made mostly of two gases, hydrogen and helium. The Sun, for example, is 74 percent hydrogen and 24 percent helium.

Local Group The 40 or so galaxies in the same general area of space as the Milky Way. The Local Group is one of many in the Virgo Supercluster.

Mass The amount of material, or matter, that makes up an object.

Milky Way The huge barred spiral of stars to which the Sun and planets belong.

Nebula A cloud of gas and dust in outer space. There are several different kinds of nebula: reflection, emission, dark, and planetary.

Plasma An electrically charged cloud of gas or dust.

Radiation The whole range of wave energy in nature, including radio waves, heat waves (infrared), x-rays, and visible light.

Satellite A space object that circles, or orbits, around a bigger one. Globular star clusters and some dwarf galaxies orbit the Milky Way, just as the planets orbit the Sun.

solar system The name for the Sun, the eight major planets, and other space objects that circle it.

Starburst galaxy A galaxy that is in a massive star-forming period.

Supernova The huge explosion of a dying giant star. For a few weeks or months, a supernova may outshine an entire galaxy, until it gradually fades from view.

This is the emission nebula NGC604. It is in the Triangulum galaxy, one of the three biggest galaxies in the Local Group.

■ GOING FURTHER

Using the Internet is a great way to expand your knowledge of space, stars, and galaxies.

Your first visit should be to the site of the U.S. space agency, NASA. Its site shows almost everything to do with space, from the history of spaceflight to the universe in general.

There are also websites that give detailed space information. Try these sites to start with:

www.nasa.gov	A huge space site.
www.space.com	Space news site.
chandra.harvard.edu	Space telescope site.
www.stellarium.org	Terrific (and free!) night sky viewing software.

■INDEX